Hungry He

Hungry Hedgehog is looking for food.

3

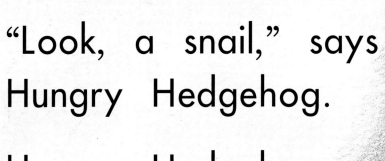

"Look, a snail," says Hungry Hedgehog.

Hungry Hedgehog likes snails.

4

5

"Look, a worm," says Hungry Hedgehog.

Hungry Hedgehog likes worms.

"Look, a beetle," says
Hungry Hedgehog.

Hungry Hedgehog
likes beetles.

8

"Look, an egg," says
Hungry Hedgehog.

Hungry Hedgehog
likes eggs.

"Look, cat food," says
Hungry Hedgehog.

Hungry Hedgehog
likes cat food.

"Go away,
Hungry Hedgehog!"
says the cat.

14

"This is my food!"